THROUGH MY EYES

A Journey in Diligent Faith

SHARON GALLOP

Through My Eyes: A Journey in Diligent Faith

Copyright © 2023 Sharon Gallop

Produced and printed by Stillwater River Publications.
All rights reserved. Written and produced in the
United States of America. This book may not be reproduced
or sold in any form without the expressed, written
permission of the author and publisher.

Visit our website at
www.StillwaterPress.com
for more information.

First Stillwater River Publications Edition

ISBN: 978-1-958217-89-4

Library of Congress Control Number: 2022923839

1 2 3 4 5 6 7 8 9 10
Written by Sharon Gallop.

Published by Stillwater River Publications,
Pawtucket, RI, USA.

The views and opinions expressed
in this book are solely those of the author
and do not necessarily reflect the views
and opinions of the publisher.

THROUGH MY EYES

Journal Chronicles
—— 2022 ——

Gifted Chronicles Daily

INSPIRATION

As I completed my grand rising prayer session my viewpoint from the bedroom window appeared to be a beautiful clear day outside. With a feeling of inspiration, I took a little trip to the other side of the city, exploring the various businesses and coffee shops. Everywhere was the hustle and grind of the community making their way through the day's appointments and schedules. Taking in the rays of the sunlight, the birds singing melodies, and the breeze of the wind, sometimes you get that split second of stillness. In a daze you acknowledge all that is around you. It's just completely amazing how God has created us all, allowing us to experience such scenery on a daily basis. We rarely get to take the time to just acknowledge all the blessings and miracles that God gives us daily and give Him thanks for that. I am truly thankful, grateful, and blessed and a testimony of his great wonders of love daily. God has a plan for us all. I'm looking forward to the transformation of my new life in my journey of faith with my Lord and Savior, Jesus Christ..

DETERMINATION

Today was another blessed day that God has provided. I was very productive and purposeful. I'm achieving my goals that I have set for myself one step at a time with God's grace each and every day. I'm so grateful and blessed that with God all things are possible; I'm a witness to the testimony of His miracle that He gave me just last week. So when you are fighting for something you're passionate about or have a vision that you want to create, no matter how hard or long it takes, it will happen. I've always had thoughts of having a higher purpose or task, of a journey to serve or to help, and to inform particularly woman and children. Over the years I have found myself doing just that, in different situations or various occasions. Somehow or somewhere in my life, I was connected to women and children in different statuses such as a single parent, a family, or a friend's family, and throughout the years the connections were all for a purpose, for me to serve, guide, and communicate all the help that I could give through the will of God . It's a beautiful experience to be blessed with the gifts of communication, understanding, compassion, wisdom, knowledge, patience, and peace. Having positive energy and feeling effective with a real purpose in someone's life is truly a pure blessing from God to be honored and, cherished and shared with others, to receive such a beautiful experience that God has given...

TIME

Time is now, very delicate time is life & death, it's everything when you feel as though you have nothing left, but do you have time still to do all that you will, it has its way of setting in that adrenaline of anxiousness to completion as I continue further in my journey the melodies of earlier pastures glide through like picture frames in my head, with sharp rhythms of what lies ahead, new beginnings of time, talk with me, take a walk in my shoes, if you will, feel the distance of historical miles taken on the bottom of my heels, as you come to a sudden stand still, time do we really have it to say I'm sorry, I care, I'm grateful, I forgive you, I love you.

TRUTH

Today a close friend of mine shared some personal inspiration she is learning to keep in her life consistently, that being in tune with a higher calling, bigger than one's self is okay, and to acknowledge that sometimes in your life you need to step away to complete an assigned journey only you can accomplish. Having that space, peace of mind, dedication, loyalty, devotion, discipline, obedience, enthusiasm, love, faith, consistency, no distractions, no drugs, no alcohol, complete surrender, complete commitment, and knowing that it is okay to shut out the distractions, lusts, evils, corruption, wickedness of the world for salvation of eternal life, and the blessing and grace of true discipline and obedience is endless. I'm truly thankful for such an amazing highlight of my day. I am also reading and learning the word of God, plugging into the source of the word of God. A complete connection with God, learning and understanding, truly and clearly who He is, and building a relationship with him and all the beautiful blessings He continues to give us each day. I'm working on understanding myself more and how to get more connected spiritually to God. I plan to be baptized for my birthday this year. It will be for the new beginning of my journey to come. It's been a very long road, but I know that with God all things are possible.

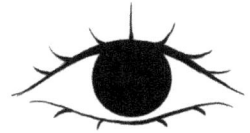

THE ASSURANCE OF SALVATION

This Grand Rising I learned about how to know and understand about the assurance of salvation. It is when we truly look within ourselves, our hearts, that we choose to want our own sins dead. Knowing what our own motivation is to put an end to all the sin in our lives, we must be led by the spirit. It kills the sin inside us. We must want it dead to glorify Him, our father. To truly be a son of God, a child of God, you must be led by the spirit if it is truly your purpose in your heart to kill your own sins. To glorify God then you are being led by the spirit and you are a son of God and a child of God. It is also said that in the book of Romans it is the complete testimony of assurance to salvation. Praying this Grand Rising gave me a lot of understanding, and assurance on where I stand in my assurance of salvation. It really helped me to know more clearly what is needed and required of me in my spirituality. The ability to get closer to God is to be led by the spirit, not of the flesh, and to live and walk in the spirit. I've also come to learn the elements of this action are also by devotion, loyalty, enthusiasm, diligence, dedication, and our commitment to God by continuing to be led by the spirit. I will triumph away from the corruption, and evils of the world by keeping my focus on God, his word, learning to live and walk by the spirit, getting to know the spirit, and establishing a communication and relationship by being led by the spirit.

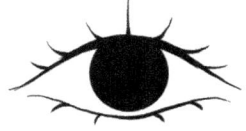

SCRIPTURE

Today I began a new book of the New Testament in the Bible, the epistle of Paul the apostle to the Romans. It is Paul's ministry of the gospel of Christ. He explains his devotion and obedience to the word of God , and the blessing and grace that He has been given to teach the gospel. In this first chapter it speaks of all truth and his longing to seek Him, God our father, and to make it known that He is not ashamed of the gospel of Christ for the gospel is the power of God to give salvation to everyone who believes. The gospel has the righteousness of God in it. I am very glad I was led to this book in the New Testament. It is very inspiring and allows me to have a better understanding of God 's will for me and I am also learning more and more of who He is. Enhancing my faith in spiritual growth in the scriptures, and also in God and Jesus Christ our savior. I am looking to grow further in a connection with God. Also, a relationship with him. I'm also learning what steps I need to take to become baptized by, or on, my birthday — a new life, mind, heart, and soul. A new life purpose. I am here to do my father's business. I choose salvation, love, peace, forgiveness, faith, devotion, loyalty, enthusiasm, diligence, discipline, and obedience to be led by the Holy Spirit, peace on earth, the restoring of the land, to change my mindset of the things of this world, and to learn to walk and live in the spirit and faith.

GOD'S PURPOSE FOR PLACEMENT

Today was a very blessed start to the day. I was so very blessed and grateful to be a part of it. I was waiting for the bus to come so I could handle some business on the other side of town, I was looking for the 76 bus to Cottage Street. Many busses came and went and it seemed like hours waiting for my bus to arrive. In the midst of all the time that passed a lot of events were going on around me. One event in particular was on the other side of the bus depot. An older man who was very intoxicated did a very disrespectful and disturbing action in front of a child. He literally exposed himself to relieve himself in front of a little girl with her mother standing right there. Unbeknownst to her, he appeared to be hurt with blood running down his face. it was stated that he was punched in the face for the action but that was misinformation. It was also said that he had fallen due to intoxication. A guy was yelling at him for his lude act in front of a child and other bus passengers were also stating how wrong he was to do that in front of a child. At that time the police came and questioned everyone about the situation. They were given the facts of the action and crime committed, but they seemed more concerned with who allegedly attacked him, not for the indecent exposure he had committed on a child in broad daylight. The mother was very disgusted and angry by this reaction in regard to her daughter. It was just crazy how they really disregarded what had just happened to a child in front of everyone. We need more effectiveness and proper justice that is served the right way. I believe she also called the police at that particular time to press charges and give her statement of what had happened, what the reaction was, and how it was handled. Our justice system has got to get better for everyone all over the world. For truth in the justice system — legal, criminal, judicial —for all the cultures, and nationalities all over the country we must allow ourselves to be led by the spirit. It is the only way to unite and save the land, love one another as God loves us. God works in mysterious ways, He is the alfa and omega for only with Him all things are possible and I'm a testimony to that. I just experienced it. He will place you where he wants you to be at any particular moment in your life. For his purpose trust in God always, get to know Him each and every day of your lifetime. Be blessed and grateful to be on that journey, getting to know Him more and more every day as you begin to really look at your surroundings, where you have been in life, and where you are now. Allow yourself that time to just be still, listen and see. You open your mind up to new surroundings and awakenings, and it's a beautiful feeling. Change your mindset, allow yourself to be led by the Holy Spirit and God will show you beautiful awakening surroundings.

A BEAUTIFUL SOUL

I stay in tune like the wind, as the current shifts out & in periodically, taking my breath like the storm of the century. Aas I stare off in a daze of atmospheres, surrounding within me, stories like Ripley's believe it or not, I reach out with the healing of the world in one shot, a screaming voice of despair goes on endlessly unheard, with the desire of letting the caged birds free with all I've got. Oh, how the soul yearns for loved ones to understand Thee, beautiful places, fairytale & fantasy, an oasis beyond me, I feel free, the surrender of sweet love reality, like the bridge over troubled waters I stand, invisible like footprints in the sand.

WEBSITE IS UP

I am so grateful and blessed for the courage, strength, and knowledge God has blessed me with to complete my website. To allow me to publish it is so amazing. I felt the gift of God's touch, inspiration, and spirit while creating my website. I know that with God all things are possible and He will make a way for success in your tasks, goals, life projects, ideas and life purpose. Keeping your eyes, mind and heart focus on Him and his word, and allowing yourself to be led by the spirit is the blessing of God and his beautiful grace that He gives to us, to keep achieving our dreams. I'm looking to inspire, uplift, motivate, challenge, and change the lives of so many to allow them to really feel the love of my artistry that I was blessed with. To know that anything they dream of achieving — a passion, a goal, a project —that when they allow themselves to be led by the spirit it will happen for them. Our God is a mighty, beautiful, merciful God. He knows our hearts, souls, and life dreams that we keep inside of us. Some are not able to express it or are afraid to express it due to the opinions of others but God said, "I will show you the way, I will give you all that you need to create all that you desire focus your eyes ,mind, heart, and soul on me." God will give everything that is needed. I am a testimony to that because He has blessed me continuously each and every day of my life. I'm so grateful for it. I am here to do my father's work, sharing the good news to all I see through my gift from God . I am so thankful it resonated within my soul when I listened to the song God sent to me for my website. It was so beautiful, it was definitely a sign at that moment that I knew my father was pleased with me for having faith in my task, goal, and life purpose and that it was meant to be completed and processed at that particular moment. I truly am grateful. I have so much more to achieve and create and I'm looking forward to making a beautiful positive change by the spirit in the lives of others. Thank you so much God, I love you and need you.

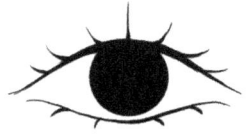

MY GOD IS ALWAYS ON TIME

Today was a good productive day. I was able to provide the new status update of my nutritional coverage in the a timely manner that was needed. With God all things are possible. It was God's will and blessing because he knows how important it is for me going forward. Thank you so much God, for guiding me in the right direction.

I miss being back home in Boston. I will revisit when the season changes to warmer weather. One thing I know for sure is that God has a plan for us all and we are going to make it through all of this with God's help. He's going to make it happen, as we allow ourselves to be led by the spirit, wonderful things are going to happen. The spirit is going to shine bright on us all as we keep our focus on God and continue to do our father's work.

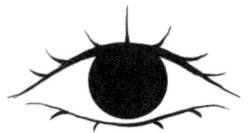

PERSISTENCE/CONSISTENCE TOWARDS MY LIFE'S PURPOSE JOURNEY

As I continue towards my task, goals, and life purpose I see a very positive future ahead allowing myself to stay focused on a tunnel vision of God. Being led by the spirit is the only way, looking to his understanding and will He has set for me to achieve. I know that the victory is already won, He is guiding me all the way to my life purpose with all that I need. I am so blessed and grateful for all that He is doing in my life daily. I now will continue to keep on creating more and more, new ideas come to me as I brainstorm exactly how I want it to be. I will stand out from the normal status that everyone is used to, bringing a completely different read to my audience, taking them in like a beautiful soothing breeze of fresh air on a sweltering hot summer day. That's what readers need, a new refreshing artistry that they are going to want all the time. I am a child of God, He is in me. I will bring the comfort, inspiration, love, motivation, hope, determination, devotion, diligence, and passion into the lives of others/artist as well with the ability to restore, and take their lives and artistry to a whole new level of their dreams. We all get one life to live but through our father, God, all things are possible. We are blessed, gifted, and we have won. We are warriors of Jesus Christ as long as we keep our focus on the FATHER, SON, and HOLY SPIRIT we are unstoppable in this lifetime.

THE POWER OF UNDER-STANDING THROUGH THE WORD OF GOD

During my prayer session a message stood out to me as I continued on my journey of spiritual growth and understanding the Holy Spirit, getting to know myself on a spiritual level, who and where I am at in my life spiritually, my faith, connection, and relationship with God . In that particular message I've learned that what we choose to allow, or accept a vice such as drugs, alcohol, and addictions to become our choice of need of escape we only allow ourselves to go deeper into our own anxieties, depression, and illusions, without the spirit of God in our lives, continuing to allow ourselves to become captives of the enemy. We don't have to worry about the types of anxieties, depressions, bondages of fear, a slave to worry. All we have to do is focus on the Holy Spirit and allow all thoughts of love, peace, happiness, joy of his forgiveness, grace, comfort, and blessings each and every day of our lives. No one is perfect, we all fall short. But when we believe in the spirit of God, we have the greatest power on earth. A man will fall to sin seven times. As long as you get back up and run to Jesus Christ our Lord and savior, He will restore you. Everything that you need is in him, therefore, if He is in you, you are in him, and you can share love with everyone you see, share the gospel with all who come around you. I'm becoming more and more aware of my surroundings in this life and the connection it has with my spirituality through the spirit of God . Be not of the things of this world but be of the spirit of God and He will show you the way that you shall go. It's been a journey. I'm so blessed and grateful for all the things God is making known and aware to me. I'm going to continue to remain focused on Him and his word and understanding.

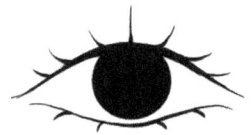

NEW WORSHIP AT FIRST BAPTIST CHURCH OF PAWTUCKET

Today is a beautiful Sunday. I am blessed and grateful I am a child of God. Today is also an inspirational day. I went to church for the first time in several years. I went to the First Baptist Church of Pawtucket not too far from my home on the other side of the city and it was a beautiful service. I was a bit early but I sat and waited for the service to begin. I met the pastor and the deacon of the church and they were very inviting. I felt a calmness, peaceful, uplifted, happiness, joyful, blessed they were welcoming, assuring me that I can enjoy and be relaxed and embrace the spirit of God and the unity with everyone in the church. Also, today's sermon was amazing cause it was in the Book of Acts1-2:13 and it resonated with my spirit cause

I remember reading that same scripture in my very own prayer and Bible session and as I listened to what the pastor was saying I was thinking, *wow*. I felt a strong feeling like I was really supposed to be there today at this time to hear that word being told, because I had said yesterday that I was determined to make it to the church to worship God and learn more and more of the gospel and my life's purpose within from the spirit of God . And it just so happened that today is a special day of the church in reference to Pentecostal, a new beginning of the church when it all first began. I hope to learn more about that as I grow in my scripture readings because it was a very interesting sermon and service. I also got a chance to talk with the pastor about my faith and my spiritual journey of where I'm trying to go and becoming baptized. He informed me that I can talk with the deacon and other members. In regard to that I will be contacted. She told me how they are starting up a baptism group session towards getting baptized and I can become involved and would be given information about the group or program they are going to have. I'm so happy that I did make it to church on this Sunday. I'm so blessed and grateful.

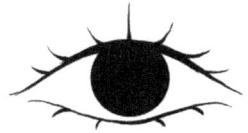

MY VISION
MY LIFE'S PURPOSE

My vision of passion is writing how I feel about my experiences of various places, people, and the causes and effects of life that I experienced, good, bad, ugly, and expressing love from my view of experience, the change of events in the world, to have a pure connection of life as it is and to be able to express that in the purest form possible. Having a pure connection with another human that when you're in their presence you can feel the energy and able to truly acknowledge them through communication. I truly believe God blessed me with a gift of the hands in which I have a love and passion for writing. Poetry being my area of artistry, I've been writing for a while now, but was slacking in my artistry and I'm not proud of that at all. Throughout the years I've been writing bits and pieces then life really stepped in and took over for a minute and the world stopped literally. It was very hard but that was the fuel to get the passion going again. I had a lot of time to think and my talent haunted me to get back on it, so that I can become the author I know that I am inside. My gift is to help heal the people of the world. Prior to the pandemic crisis I had a chance to express my writing in front of strangers and fellow artists like myself young and old and I got a feedback memo from one of them that resonates with me till this day. I hope to someday come in contact, or connection with that young person that saw the gift of talent that God blessed me with way back when, to let her know it's been some years later, and I'm still passionate about my talent and I don't have to be afraid to express anything that God has blessed me with. I see myself signing books at a bookstore, and on a TV talk show talking about my books cause I'm going to take my talent by God and create a beautiful gospel poetry book with his guidance and blessing.

AFFIRMING YOUR VISION

Today was a day of recognition in oneself a particular area of the mindset, owning every area of your life learning and acknowledging the love for yourself, doing for yourself, also putting yourself first, and excepting that it's okay to allow yourself to be put first. The biggest step in self-love is learning, and understanding who you are and accepting it. Affirming Clarity in your Vision, in your life, knowing who you are, what you're doing, and why you're doing it and how you're doing it, day by day, moment by moment. Under no circumstances second guess your own clarity of your Vision. Never judge your own clarity based on other people's response. Affirm Your Vision every day, changing your mindset using the "I AM" battle strike each and every day against the enemy. I am a powerful child of God, I Am the righteousness of God, I Am Blessed, I Am wealthy, abundant, I Am healed, with God all things are possible.

CITY VIBEZ

Today was a good day with the average hustles and grind of the week, but for some reason it seemed as though everyone was more busy than normal, moving about everywhere a lot more than usual. I'm thinking it has to do with our cities and state of Rhode Island going back to one hundred percent capacity of daily living in public restaurants, bars, beaches, gyms, libraries, hospitals, churches, markets. As our communities in various states begin to live again, gain back the resources, we need to complete our day-to-day tasks and responsibilities, to take care of our children, family, relatives, friends, neighbors, citizens, to have the freedom to move about freely and safely. Spring is in full bloom. Summer is on its way. I will be led by the Holy Spirit to enjoy all the great blessings that He continues to give every day. I will continue to live in love, peace, and happiness in the understanding of the Holy Spirit and his word each and every day and sharing that love with everyone I know and I meet. The kingdom of God is Authority.

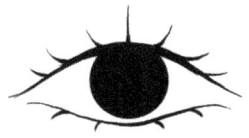

GOD CHOOSES

Today was a very still, calm day, a time to reflect about the chain of events of the week. All the various tasks, appointments, functions, taking in all the experiences and actions of our lives. As you're moving about you rarely get to take that time needed to just be still for a minute. You feel as though you have to keep going taking care of all your daily and weekly tasks and goals you want to create and complete. With God all things are possible. With any dream you have you can go above and beyond no matter how far or how long it may seem. I feel as though there is a message within the stillness of this day. God uses the foolish things to confound the wise and the weak things of the world to shame the strong. God can use a humble heart and an underdog who has been counted out by the world is God's favorite vessel.

KEEPING THE PEACE

It is a very important position to keep the peace in various situations when it comes to the public, society, family, relatives, children, friends, colleagues, and neighbors. Speaking from many experiences of maintaining peace in disruptive situations in this world right now, not everyone wants anything to do with peace. All they want is revenge or chaos and destruction. When you allow your mind to be consumed with confusion, anxiety, hatred, and fear it creates a storm of anger in your subconscious and that's all you see, hear, and think. It becomes a complete dominion over your mind as you continue to lose more and more of yourself looking for release of satisfaction. Instead, you only sink deeper into your own realm of consuming hatred and anger inside, which is now out of your control, into a state of exhaustion and emptiness. But God wants us to channel within our Godliness of wisdom to bring about peace unto others. We can respectfully confront anyone whom we feel may have done us wrong or hurt us mentally, or verbally. With God's love we can return that love to others that hurt or cause us pain, sorrow, or discomfort. God sees and knows all, He is everywhere. We don't even know He gives us the grace to change the course of any situation that disrupts the peace in this world and many times saved lives by doing so. Every heart matters. Rely on the Godly wisdom inside of you to keep the peace as much as we can day by day, moment by moment. It could mean the difference between life or death.

LOVE

Love is the essential core of our very existence, a very powerful emotion that resonates within the core of our being. It's so often misunderstood, misused, abused, and misrepresented. If we take the time to learn and understand the pureness and truth in love we then will begin to adapt to the divine nature of its existence beyond our imagination and the powerful abilities that it holds within us. But we must be aware and open to its very existence to acquire complete access to it. It is a force that is bigger than us. But when we allow ourselves that force of energy we will then realize that it is all around us, it has been year after year, season after season, a beautiful scenery of love all over the nation, country, cities and states. Love rejoices in truth, for God so loved the world that He gave his only begotten son, that He who so ever believeth in Him shall not perish but shall have everlasting life.

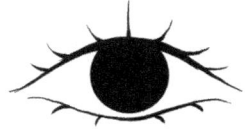

HEALING

In this Grand Rising 's prayer and scripture reading God reminds us that we do not have to be fearful or distraught in any situation that we may be facing in that moment. He assures us to rely on Him and strength will be given to us. Faith is a key factor in our daily lives as we continue to struggle and fight all the evils of this world. We must allow ourselves to be led by the spirit daily and feed on the word of God to grow stronger in our faith and spirituality, and the Holy Spirit. With God all things are possible, in the scriptures of the old and new testaments God has the power to heal our physical bodies, beautiful, amazing healings in this life that we live. Feed on the word of God, tell Him your pain and hurt in every aspect of your life and He will restore and make your life whole again.

GOD'S PATH FOR US

We must trust in the Lord, with all our hearts letting Him lead us on the path He has chosen for us. Keeping our focus and acknowledgment on Him daily, He will give all that we need to achieve tasks, goals, dreams, and our life purpose. Staying strong, devoted, loyal, and diligent in the word of God , by being led by the spirit daily and changing our mindset, growing, learning in our faith and spirituality by being consistent on our spiritual journey is our number one priority. Our Heavenly Father knows that we as believers will fall short, as long as we get back up and run to Him, directly humbling ourselves before Him, and ask for forgiveness our father is a kind and loving God. He understands, sees, and knows all things. When we come before our father with our pure state of mind, body, heart, and soul our connection with God is blessed and acknowledged. We as believers must continue to help others to continue to seek the understanding of God and His will. The kingdom of God is authority.

A DAY OF RESOLVE

The Grand Rising was very calm. It was a day of relaxing, releasing, and resolving any and all burdens of stress, concern, worry, upset anger, disappointment, temptation and the causes and effects that life brings our way daily. These are the roadblocks, obstacles, confusion, and misdirection that the enemy is always putting in our path when He realizes that we are moving forward towards good, and understanding the love and will of God. Oh, he does not like that. So, he creates these disturbances in our daily lives to get us off the track of our goals, understanding, and life's purpose, and the path that God has created for us. But we as the children of God can shut all of that down by fighting the enemy back harder with the mighty word of God, letting go, and letting God fight all your battles, fear, stress, anger, and upset. He will turn it all around into a beautiful blessing of love, strength, knowledge, and wisdom for the journey of your life's purpose.

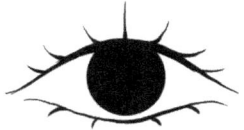

RAIN

Today it is raining out with some lightening and there was a big thunder bolt that set off a car alarm. Whenever I see rain, I think of the cleansing of the earth, peace, the beauty of nature, how the rain flows down through the trees bringing a cool mist of air with a sense of calm and relaxation, being in tune with all that is around you, the melody of the birds and the trees swaying and singing in the wind. Everyone is in their home taking care of their children, husbands, wives, taking care of the household, preparing a hearty meal for the family, also family time or a movie night. The rain brings out a beautiful feeling of togetherness among families and friends. On rainy days of calm and relaxation fill your mind and heart with warmth, love, comfort, peace, joy and happiness. It is all through the beautiful gift and blessing and grace of God, only with God all things are possible.

GOD SAID BE NOT AFRAID FOR I AM WITH THEE

As the day continues, the trees are swaying to a steady wind. I see the swiftness of the birds taking flight in various areas high above the trees all around, the beauty and activity of nature that we see every day, but we don't take the time to just acknowledge it as we should. As I continue to grow, learn, and acknowledge new experiences that occur in my life God has been bringing certain things to my awareness in regard to people, places, and situations. He places you into particular instances to show you that He is always with you, and that you don't have to fear. He also tests your faith in various aspects of your life. It is the very core of your spirituality fighting though and against the temptations of this world. But knowing through the word of God that love conquers all fears, doubt, hatred, and temptation, and keeping our focus on Him and His word, feed on his word and continue to change your mindset. Allow yourself to be led by the spirit, (the Holy Spirit) learning and understanding how to walk and talk in the spirit, look to the understanding of God and his will, He will guide your path.

GOD SAID DO NOT GIVE WHAT IS HOLY TO THE DOGS

Today I learned that it is very important to know and understand that you were made in the likeness and image of God, and understand the authority and power you're walking in daily. You are the divine one, the chosen one, of God, by God, from God . God wants us to come to this knowledge, taking action to be transformed by the renewing of your mind. It's the only way to know what God's will is, the only way to know what your calling is, the only way that you're going to see that you are priceless. God says do not cast your pearls before swine, the blessing of the Lord makes rich and it adds no sorrow to it. Keeping your focus and you're understanding on him, tell him your troubles, give him the praise and glory for all that He does in your life. Rely on the Lord only, put your trust and faith in him and He will deliver all that you shall need and more. Keep your presence in the likeness of the Lord and continue to be led by the spirit daily, walking and talking in the spirit daily.

A TIME TO TRIUMPH

In this new month the days have already started full speed ahead, with various tasks, appointments, required events, and goals. It will definitely be a very productive month. I'm looking forward to new acknowledgements, changes, and beginnings in every aspect of my life. This has been a challenging year, but with a bright future ahead, and the right focus and diligence going forward, the path to achievement is unstoppable. With the focus and understanding of God 's will everything is possible, I'm letting God take the lead in my life. He will guide my path as I continue my journey in faith, spirituality, and life purpose and also helping others to seek refuge in him, to experience the beautiful blessing that He gives us each and every day. I am so grateful and blessed, I love my Heavenly Father and I need him daily.

RE-CONNECTING (FAITH, DISCIPLINE, AND OBIDENCE)

Today I'm so thankful, grateful and blessed for all that God continues to do for me each and every day of my life. He has reawakened a beautiful strength, motivation, fire, will, discipline, and obedience in this warrior of Christ. With diligence, determination of faith, prayer, worship, and scripture I am being led by the Holy Spirit daily to reconnect with the word of God . I have been on a spiritual journey, and there is a powerful spiritual warfare going on, but I know and believe that God has plans for my life in this lifetime. I hadn't been to worship in a few weeks and I wasn't good with that at all. I felt I needed to hear and experience the presence of God 's direction and guidance effective immediately. As I acknowledge and learn more and more about the word of God, I see things differently, and feel differently. I have been feeling the need to remove myself from certain situations, places, and people in regard to family, relatives, friends, and neighbors alike. I know that I made a change in my life for a purpose and I'm growing and learning in that purpose. It's a life-altering decision that I choose to make, that I want for my life, and I'm going to continue keeping my focus on God (my father)and his word. I have given my life to Christ, my Lord and Savior and I'm learning how to live as He would want me to live in love, faith, righteousness, and peace, and to tell all the good news. It is a journey and process when you choose salvation, to be renewed, delivered, and made whole again. That's what my life journey is about, learning to put God first in your daily life, unapologetic and unashamed. I am so blessed and thankful for my blessings that my father continues to give even when I fall short. Well, I'm running to Jesus in my darkest, hardest, and happiest times. He is always on time every time we need him. I'm so thankful God blessed me with the determination and the will to get up and come to him, to worship, cause I truly need him in my life, with so much going on around me. Within my daily life I need him so much. I love Him and I can't do it without Him. I thank you Lord for your blessing, love, and grace in my life.

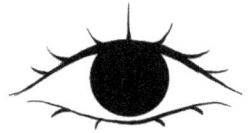

A NEW BOOK CHAPTER IN CORINTHIANS

As I read this Grand Rising's scripture, I was thankful to get a new understanding of what was being said — the parables of the last supper, also the final instructions, personal plans, and greetings. Now each scripture has a significant meaning and message. It was very informative; it just opens your mind to a new way of thinking and acknowledgement of how we ought to live amongst the land and how we should treat one another. I just know that I want to walk and talk in the spirit daily and be transformed by the renewing of my mind, and help others to do the same. I will have to get out of this controlled mindset that I'm in, and completely allow myself to be led by the spirit daily. I can do it. I will do it. I am going to do it. I'm going to get back up. I'm going to run my race. God loves me. I am the righteousness of God, I am abundant, I am wealthy, I am healed, I am blessed, I am the creative force of the universe. With God all things are possible. I know my God will guide me all the way.

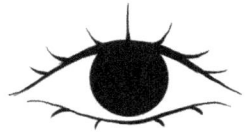

HELPFUL SUNDAY

It was a very moveable day for a Sunday as I started with my Grand Rising prayer and scriptures. It was interesting and had me thinking for a minute. When you read that Bible it takes you to another world as you understand what is really being said. You begin to feel as though you're there. It's so amazing, you're really drawn into the word of God , and as I continue to seek and read it more and more, I continue to acknowledge, learn, and understand. All the stories are beautiful, as well as sad, informative, empowering, uplifting, and joyful. It just puts your mind into a different perspective on life and it's truly amazing. I truly want to get in my new space, and cleanse my mind, heart, and soul of all this programed, corrupt, evil, wicked world and just focus on the renewal of my mindset and the beautiful word of God and my savior's way of living. I'm going to make that a reality in my new season with the guidance of my father and Lord and savior.

ANGEL IN THE CLOUDS

Today was a very meaningful day. I had a good Grand Rising start with a beautiful prayer and devotional session. It was inspiring and informative regarding how God's love for us is so divine and how much He wants us to walk and talk in His light. The more I read the more exciting and interesting it became. I just need stronger discipline to keep focused on the word of God . It's truly amazing. Also, within the midst of my day I believe that God may have answered my question I asked in a prayer. I asked a specific question to God pertaining to the parish that I have been going to, the one I had recently found (the First Baptist church of Pawtucket). As the second half of my day continued, a lady had come to me, a God -fearing woman, and she explained about a church service happening this Sunday online via zoom at 11:30 am. I truly believe that it's a testament to my prayer. My God is a loving and caring God, also a true God , and He will show you and get you what you need every time. It may not happen when you want it to or expect it to, but when it does it's right on time when it's supposed to happen. I'm so thankful and grateful for all that He does for me daily in my life. Also, I continued to venture outbound. There were a lot of different events going on in various sections of the city, a very busy afternoon but so beautiful outside with nature flowing and swaying from the cool breeze in the air. Something within brought my attention to the sky and in the sky there were an amazing cloud formation that was so mind boggling it left me in awe of what I was seeing. It was the heavenly formation of an angel with wings so elegant it was all I could do was get completely lost in what I was seeing. That's how much of a trance of inspiring, exciting, amazement I was in seeing such a heavenly scene of the most beautiful clouds ever.

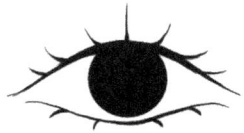

SEPTEMBER FALL SEASON

This is a new month, a new season, one of the good ones. Positive Vibez, energy, thoughts, communication, people — it's a fresh start with a clearer view to new beginnings. I am thankful and grateful for all that I have. I am going to work on being stronger in every aspect of my life, in this life, faith, prayer, worship, scripture, the Holy Spirit, a beacon of light for all to see the beauty of our Lord and Savior and how He continues to bless us each and every day. I will become better than I was yesterday and keep my focus on God no matter what the temptation is to throw me off course. I am going to stay the path that I am supposed to travel. It's going to be an amazing sight to see the trees' transformation when the full bloom of fall begins to take over. Various colors in nature's fall scenery are such a good vision like cozy fall nights as the weather shifts with the season. Time for hoodies and sweaters, getting up to assist kids going off to school first thing in the morning even before you have your morning coffee, it's the hustle and bustle of the new school year in person. Now that the majority of kids are able to have vaccinations, parents are slowly returning back to work full and part time. Lord, give us the strength and power to come together and find a better solution other than destruction and murder amongst our children, create within them a clean heart, a clean spirit, and freedom from bondage of all types. Help them find their way within the light of salvation. It's such a beautiful day after a tremendous amount of rain that caused floods in different areas of the city and also various other states causing severe water damage and power outages. I know the cities and states have utility crews all over the region doing all that they can to restore power and help with weather damage. This season is going to be beautiful, blessed, and protected.

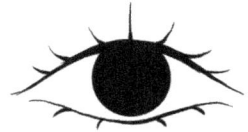

PRODUCTIVE

When you wake up to the beautiful sunrays in the morning with nature, birds, and trees swaying about you have to stop in your tracks and thank God for such an amazing day He has blessed us with. Also, for having the strength and determination to do what needs to be done and making the right choices in various aspects of your life guided by God . He is everywhere even when you don't think He is there. I can testify to that cause today He did just that for me, showing me that I had what I needed to get the task done that I needed to complete. I thank you God for giving me the diligence to achieve it. Although summer is gone, we still have the beautiful clear sky and dry weather as fall moves forward full speed ahead. The nights are getting a bit chilly very fast. It is Labor Day weekend so the cities are going to be very busy with parties, barbeques, and events. I wish for a great time for everyone — friends, relatives, and neighbors — to be able to celebrate and enjoy the holy day in peace and love with good times and vibes. As the month continues rolling along I see new strengths, achievements, confidence, challenges accomplished, new ideas, transformation, and change. It's a beautiful thing when you can find the power to stay focused no matter what gets in your way to distract you and God just keeps on working right through you. That light is too bright within to ever be dimmed. It's overflowing on the outside, attracting and embracing others with curiosity. Oh, my God is a mighty loving God, always on time. I thank you Heavenly Father for your continuous love and protection daily.

HEAVY EMOTION

It came over me in a surge, a smothering
   of multiple emotions, all at once.
Like an instant earthquake, when it's too late
   to make any decisions
Or moves, taking it all in, looking for
   an answer as it's happening.
Why at this moment, what is the meaning in it,
    where is the solution?
It's heavy
My body & bones are tight,
   my mind is an erupting volcano.
All the possibilities of cause & effects
   of this sudden pressure,
Of emotions from various elements,
Turning points of current events in this life.
My life, family, friends, strangers, sports,

Entertainment, politics, world hunger.
It's heavy.
Out of control, as it destroys the hopes & dreams of unity,
Humanity is fighting to stay alive, separation of nations.
Boulders of thoughts roll like rivers through my mind,
Of the answer to the suffering of
    these ferocious, breathtaking,
Everlasting, impatient, tragic,
    heartbreaking emotion's.
It's heavy.

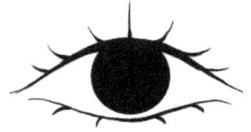

PERSISTENCE MOTIVATION AND DETERMINATION

Today was very productive as I continue to prepare for the relocation process. I started the removal of unneeded items in my apartment. Now is the time for the re-examination of forms, letters, junk mail, electronics, movies, music, and games and getting everything checked and organized for relocation. I'm only about three quarters of the way done. There will be a lot of paperwork and letters to clean up. It's going to be a process but I'm on the job cause I'm ready to move on as soon as possible. I also got out for a bit and moved about the city. It was refreshing; the air and wind were singing and swaying throughout the whole day along with the birds and the beautiful silhouettes of the clouds in the sky. It was the perfect time to look up in amazement and enjoy how excited, joyful, and peaceful it made me feel. Just the sight of it helped me picture myself in my new space and environment on my balcony or patio sitting out and looking up in a beautiful daydream I got lost in. That's how joyful it felt and with the air and wind flowing it was truly beautiful. Thank you Heavenly Father for that beautiful, amazing feeling and experience that you blessed me with as a vision.

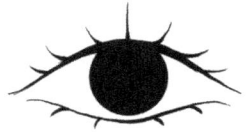

GOD BROKE YOUR FALL

Today's prophetic word was right on time. I can definitely resignate with it. I experienced the blessing of healing from God when I was in a vehicle a few Sundays ago. I am a true testimony to an amazing miracle that my Heavenly Father blessed me with. I am so thankful, grateful, and blessed and I give Him all the praise and glory for that amazing anointing that He has given me. I'm under attack these days but I'm going to fight harder with the armor of Christ and defeat the enemy cause I know that with God all things are possible, and no weapon formed against me shall prosper. God loves me. I am the righteousness of God, I am abundant, I am wealthy, I am healed, I am blessed, thank you, Heavenly Father. I love you and need you to help me to continue to grow stronger in keeping my eyes, ears, mind, and heart focused on you and your word.

HAPPY BIRTHDAY

Today is my birthday of fifty years. I am so thankful, grateful, and blessed to still be here in existence. It's been a very long road, but I have acknowledged, learned a lot about the differences in the experiences of life in this lifetime, and I am still learning and growing within the realm. As I continue towards the next phase of a new chapter in my life I am preparing for a new environment of space, going a lot further in getting to know me more than ever, growing stronger within my mindset, being transformed by the renewing of my mind, also in my faith, prayer, scripture, and worship. It's a beautiful experience getting to know my Heavenly Father, and learning how to stay strong and keep my focus on him and his word no matter what comes my way. Being led by the spirit daily, learning to walk and talk by the spirit, I'm pursuing my purpose in this lifetime with my Heavenly Father's lead. It has been a very long journey but with my continued fight against the enemy I will triumph in becoming renewed, restored, delivered, and made whole, and connecting with other warriors of Christ to help others that wants to choose salvation and help all those that allow us too. I thank you my Lord and Savior and Heavenly Father for this beautiful, blessed day you have blessed me with to receive.

THE TRUTH

I am the beginning & end of the omega,
My existence is the soul's true face, I am its sanity,
If lost I cannot be replaced, some want me, some need me,
But some also deceive me, why must they forsake me,
Believe in me & you will be cleansed, mind, body & soul.
So free like the great sea, come to me, I'll be your serenity.
With me you are complete, I am everything you desire.
I am the lifeforce of your existence, like your heartbeat.
So, when you feel you're at the end of the rope with no hope,
Just count on me & I will be there,
I am now & forever the truth.

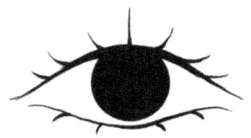

MIRRORS OF THE SOUL SHED TEARS

Looking through the mirrors of the soul you will understand the truth being told, the fight through the trials and tribulations of the daily lives of the young and the old in this life. As the rush of the day and the caution of the night awaits us, the mirrors of the soul shed tears for today and tomorrow, happiness and sorrow.

The weeping soul,
The young & the old
Peace & harmony
Mirrors that have stories that have never been told
The sick & the weak
Freedom
World Peace

SHARON GALLOP

So, whenever you are far or near, by glance or steer
To you it will be very clear
For every ocean tide that comes & goes
Whenever the wind blows
You will know
Why mirrors of the soul shed tears

INFORMATIVE INFORMATION

Today I acquired information in regard to starting a business via restaurant or food truck. The city of Pawtucket has rules, regulations, and requirements that have to be done before a business permit can be received. That was very good to know, so I'm preparing the knowledge that I received and transferring it to a new objective of new movement towards my personal tasks and goals. It was such a beautiful day out today, nature was so alive and vibrant singing a beautiful melody throughout the day. I took a walk to the Dollar ;Tree with a friend to pick up a gift item and a household item for cooking. It was a long day but a very productive one. A lot of people were out and about, spending time with family and friends, and children enjoying the blessed day that God has blessed us with. It's been a very busy week with a lot of things going on all around in various areas, good and bad, but with the power of God I am the righteousness of God. God loves me and He is with me, always helping me to break free of fear and be bold and continue to grow stronger in my focus on him and his word. Being content with being by yourself, confident, motivated, courageous, in my purpose.

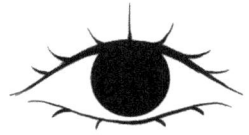

PUSHING ON AND DETERMINATION

Today with a little more patience I got more of the paperwork from years ago emptied out. Now I can check and remove the rest and also all the other miscellaneous items in the process of preparing the house for relocation. I truly hope that I can find what I'm looking for in a new space and place to call home again, to truly be comfortable and live free, and enjoy my dwelling area of living. I have so many ideas for my new chapter in my new home one of these months soon. I'm trying to keep as busy as possible and work on my purpose that God has required of me to do. I just hope I'm on the right path to do that cause I want to serve in the right way by being transformed by the renewing of my mind. I just want to feel a whole new pure vibration of positive energy, the blessing of being led by the spirit daily, and walking and talking in the spirit. It's a beautiful truth to know that it is possible with the power of our Heavenly Father's blessings, strength, and love daily. I'm going to fight through all the temptations of this world and be on the front lines of battle of all this evil and wickedness and conquer it with the mighty armor of my Lord and Savior in the fight for righteousness and salvation. Thank you Lord and my Heavenly Father for always being with me though the storms of life. No matter what I go through you will never leave me, I love you and need you always.

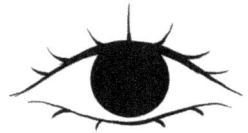

REFLECTION AND NETWORKING

Today was a lot cooler than the last few days as the month continues on. The holidays are right around the corner with so much going on all around the cities and states. I just wish the best for everyone and all the families across the nation. It's been a very hard, sad, and tragic year but I know for sure that with God all things are possible no matter what the circumstances. I contacted a few rental properties and private landlords in reference to availability for homes or apartments for rent. I'm looking to move at the right time and in the right neighborhood and financial means. It's been a long time coming. I feel that this is my season for change and I must continue to keep my focus on my Heavenly Father to guide me in the right direction towards my life's purpose. I just want to please him and gain the ability to help my family like I want to. I have to at least complete and accomplish my goals and passion to help others towards a positive place of light and love and salvation. As I continue to learn and grow in my journey of faith and spirituality acknowledging my true self and understanding, accepting, and embracing my true inner being. I have to relocate myself to a position of clean, clear, quiet vibrations, energies, and true believers of righteousness (God).

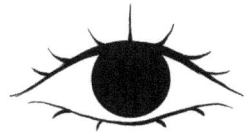

WINTER STORM WHITEOUT 2022

Looking outward into the oasis of my surroundings, engulfed in a sphere of endlessness. Do you hear that? The fierce roaring of the wind in silk layers of thick mists as the currents of the air shift and the branches on the tree bark sway about with beautiful emotions. The scenery is a Winter Wonderland of amazement in the transformation of the seasons. How we eagerly anticipate summer, spring, winter, and fall, unaware of the relentlessness of them all that is reaved to us year after year. And yet we are given the grace and glory of God. Showing us what he is capable of, bringing forth an effective state of mind, and a very direct sense of stillness that is more than often needed but we never have or find the time to take. Other than a no other choice situation resulting in the realization of the importance of how that is so much needed in the lives of so many, to awaken and acknowledge the major steps in this life's journey that's necessary for growth in perseverance in all that we do daily. It is all through the wisdom, love, and guidance of God that he shows us every day, that we open our eyes and breathe.

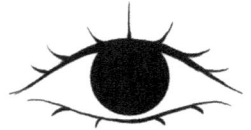

THE DAYS JOURNEY

What a day it was today. I went to check out a few things on the far side of the state in Woonsocket. I stopped in Walmart to see if they had a few items that I was looking to get. They had every other size or item but the one I wanted, and also crazy prices for those items with not much product available. It's becoming consistent at this point, making it more and more difficult to shop for the products and food items that you would like to buy or need. On the other end of things, it's crazy how the holidays are right around the corner for family, relatives, and friends gathering in a festive union of communication, a great holiday meal, conversation, laughs, and cries and good ole togetherness amongst family and friends. We need so much to come together and remind one another how much we mean to each other and how our presence is needed. Showing and sharing love, peace, and positive energy is always the key to beautiful times with beautiful people and the love and blessings of God that we receive daily is the greatest gift of all.

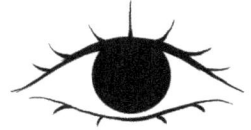

VETERANS DAY

Today is the day that we as citizens of the United States of America honor our veterans of the armed forces. So many men and women have pledged their lives to honor, serve, fight, and protect this country. So many families have endured the hardships of loved ones being away for so many years. In serving all over the world, experiences beyond our imagination of battles fought, some conquered, some defeated, but with faith, strength, determination, motivation, honor, confidence, and courage to continue on tour after tour is an amazing gift of perseverance, and triumph in the lives of these men and women making the choice to serve and protect our country throughout all that we face in this country, We still will stand united in faith to serve, heal, honor, and protect our country, the United States.

RAIN AND CLOUDY

Today I woke up (thank you Lord) to a rainy Grand Rising that suddenly turned to clouds. The wind and trees are moving abruptly and the temp is very chilly due to the rain. It's still beautiful scenery with nature being so alive and vibrant on this cold, cloudy fall day that our Heavenly Father has granted us and has blessed us with this Grand Rising. I look forward to being better than I was yesterday, keeping my focus on my Heavenly Father and his word, working on being more disciplined, and obedient, continuing to have faith, and hoping and learning to allow myself to be led by the Holy Spirit daily, walking in the spirit, talking in the spirit. I'm looking to becoming restored, renewed, delivered, and made whole.

A FIGHT AGAINST ALL ODDS

I came through to this world ready to explore and conquer all things possible. I was a lonely one due to the struggles being faced in that timeline of life, so I absorbed, fought, and embraced all of the trials and tribulations of events that I had to endure. I had to maintain strength, and courage through all of the hurt and pain in the absence of love, protection, and nurturing. Also, the stability I needed to make it through that particular storm of my life, as I continued forward from the realms of my childhood into adulthood.

It seemed as though my life as I've known it was on the continuing struggling path as an altering chain reaction from the past. I had a desperation, and the insight of a road to a positive light, but no means to get there. I was in need of a sign from heaven for a breakthrough evolution of new sight, and strength of motivation in mobility of a new direction towards a greater life. GOD has given me a divine gift of power to achieve all that is possible. Within my ability of determination with all that is against me, I choose to continue to cherish all that I have keeping my family united, and the children fed and educated. I am a warrior in this great battle of the world that we face daily. The day is coming for a completely victorious and triumphant defeat in this war. My family and their children will soar to all new heights of multiple achievements in the new world. A generation of positive change life and peace on earth, as well as their children will continue on the amazing journey toward a new path.

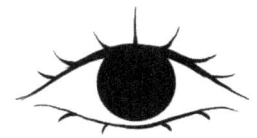

WHO CARES?

Who cares about the way the people of the world are living, who cares about the Ones that are & are not giving, who cares about the ones that's sinning, who cares about the fucked-up shit we've been in for 400 years,
But who cares
Who cares about who's lying, who cares about the babies crying, who cares about who's trying?
But who cares
Who cares about our daughters, who care about our sons, who cares for our newborn ones?
But who cares
Who cares about the true faces we hide, who cares when we laugh, we cry inside, who cares that we are Always wondering why?
But who cares
Who cares about the ones who want what's real, who cares

we bite our Tongue from saying what we truly feel, who cares about the tainted one of a pure heart steals?
But who cares
Who cares when love turns to rage, who cares when you have to keep turning the page to a brand-new chapter in your life to keep from living trifle, who cares about the circle of life?
But who cares
Who cares how we want what we can't have, that we settle for less, who cares how we are subjected to second best.
But who cares
Who cares about the pain we have to swallow, who cares about our sorrow, who cares whether we live or die tomorrow?
But who cares
Who cares if what I wrote is fact or fiction, who cares if the ones that read
this will listen, who cares that if we don't pay attention in America, we will be forever trapped in the mind of our prison, but can someone please tell me?
Who cares

www.ingramcontent.com/pod-product-compliance
Lightning Source LLC
Chambersburg PA
CBHW070306100426
42743CB00011B/2367